LOVING GOD *with all my*
STRENGTH

My grace is sufficient for you,

for my power is made perfect in weakness.

2 Corinthians 12:9

Julie Ackerman Link

Loving God with All My Strength
© 2007 Julie Ackerman Link

Discovery House Publishers is affiliated with RBC Ministries, Grand Rapids, MI 49501.

Requests for permission to quote from this book should be directed to: Permissions Department, Discovery House Publishers, P.O. Box 3566, Grand Rapids, MI 49501.

Also available in the Loving God Series:

> The Art of Loving God
> Loving God with All My Heart
> Loving God with All My Soul
> Loving God with All My Mind

For more information visit Discovery House Publishers on the Web: http://www.dhp.org/

Part of the section titled "The Strength of My Life: Integrity" is adapted from the introduction, written by Julie Ackerman Link, to Our Daily Bread: A Selection of Daily Readings from the Popular Devotional, © 1997 by Discovery House Publishers. Used by permission of Discovery House Publishers, Grand Rapids, MI 49501.

Cover Photo: Getty Images

Printed in the United States of America

07 08 09 10 11 12 13 / JRC / 10 9 8 7 6 5 4 3 2 1

Introduction

The first time I saw the Dead Sea I was startled by its beauty. It stretched before me like a sparkling array of diamonds strewn across a shimmering blue cloth. But the glittering beauty of the Dead Sea does not draw eager crystal collectors to its shoreline. The crystals that make the Dead Sea shimmer are salt. And while salt certainly has its place and purpose—it's great for enhancing the taste of food and keeping it from spoiling—we don't make jewelry out of it. No woman I know would be pleased to receive an engagement ring with a sodium chloride crystal substituting for a gemstone.

Why are women so fussy? Well, for one thing, salt today is common and cheap. Used as a symbol of love, that's what salt would say to a woman about her worth.

Diamonds on the other hand are not cheap. Finding

3

them, recovering them, and cutting and polishing them is a long and costly process. When they are finally mounted in a setting of precious metal, they become a symbol used by millions to communicate enduring love and priceless value.

Diamonds are beautiful and valuable gemstones, but the process of becoming diamonds is anything but glamorous. They start as common carbon—black, dirty, and combustible. But through countless years of intense heat and high pressure deep within the earth, they become pure and strong. This makes them a good metaphor for spiritual strength, for God uses intense outside forces to rid us of our impurities and to perfect His strength in us.

When I started writing this, I was regaining physical strength after several months of chemotherapy and radiation. During that time, I learned more than I ever wanted to know about physical weakness. But as I regained physical strength, I felt my emotional strength drying up. An unexpected event caused me to question my purpose and value. Then, as I was finishing the writing, a truly minor event plunged me into a state of emotional weakness that caught me off guard. My reservoir of emotional strength had run dry. I pleaded with God to spare me from experiencing the same level of emotional weakness that I had suffered physically one year earlier.

One thing I know, I hate feeling weak! I prefer the illusion of strength to the reality of weakness. But the truth is, we all are weak and totally dependent on God. Some of us live in places where we have few reminders of this reality. We are able to structure our lives in ways that create an illusion of self-sufficiency. But sudden loss of health, income, employment, prestige, or a treasured

5

relationship is a startling reminder of our complete dependence on God.

Despite many lessons, I still need to learn that God's strength is made perfect in my weakness. The how and why remain a mystery to me, but Jesus set the example, for He is able "to sympathize with our weaknesses" (Hebrews 4:15). What seemed to be the ultimate act of weakness—submitting Himself to a humiliating death—turned out to be His act of greatest strength.

The fiery furnace of suffering—whether physical or emotional, whether persecution from without or humiliation from within—removes our impurities and makes us strong.

When I started studying the Greatest Commandment, I assumed that loving God with all my strength had to do with physical strength and was related to concepts

script

Re: Jesus

crpt

like courage and obedience. But the word translated "might" or "strength" in Deuteronomy 6:5 is an adverb used to express "great degree or quantity: very, greatly, exceedingly, much." It signifies intensity. Like an exclamation point at the end of the command, it urges us to commit every desire of our heart, every breath of our soul, every thought and attitude of our mind to the praise and glory of God.

Whatever you do, work
at it with all your heart, as
working for the Lord . . .

—Colossians 3:23

The Strength of My Heart | Certainty

At the military museum in Istanbul, visitors can hear some of the earliest military music. The Ottomans claimed to be the first to send troops off to war accompanied by musicians. However, the Ottoman Empire didn't begin until 1299, and the biblical record indicates that Jehoshophat, king of Judah, used music in battle during his reign thousands of years earlier (c.873–849 B.C.).

Jehoshophat knew that his army was powerless to defend the small kingdom against a vast army coming to attack them, so he gathered the people together at the temple of the Lord and pleaded with God for help. He ended his prayer with these words: "We do not know what to do, but our eyes are upon you" (2 Chronicles 20:12). By acknowledging his own weakness, Jehoshophat made room for God's strength.

God answered quickly but not directly. He sent his response by way of Jahaziel the priest, a descendant of Asaph, a songwriter and worship leader. <u>Through Jahaziel</u>, the <u>Lord said to Jehoshophat</u>, "<u>Do not be afraid</u> or <u>discouraged</u> . . . <u>the battle is not yours, but God's</u>" (v. 15). ✱

2 chroN 20:15

Jehoshaphat's response was two-fold. First, he worshiped (v. 19). Second, he appointed worship singers to lead the army. <u>Before the battle even began, the service of praise and thanksgiving started</u>. As they sang "Give thanks to the LORD, for his love endures forever," the LORD set ambushes against the invaders, and they were defeated.

The difference between the Ottomans and the people of Judah is notable. Whereas the Ottomans used music to

And whatever you do, whether in word or deed, do it all in the name of the Lord Jesus, giving thanks to God the Father through him.

—Colossians 3:17

9

lift the spirits of soldiers, the Israelites used music to lift praise to the Lord.

As we learn from Jehoshaphat, the purpose of praise is not to energize or empower ourselves, but to express our confidence in God's love and power. However, having said that, the by-product of praise is that it *does* energize us. Praise proclaims our steadfast trust in God's good intentions and in His ability to right the world's wrongs even when it appears as if His side is losing. When we affirm this truth with our mouths, we hear it with our ears, and it starts a spiritual process that is like the physical process of blood circulating in our veins. When we praise God for His strength, we are strengthened. By

Be joyful always; pray continually; give thanks in all circumstances, for this is God's will for you in Christ Jesus.

—1 Thessalonians 5:16-18

acknowledging God's strength, we realize our strength in Him.

The phenomenon surrounding the publication of the book *Prayer of Jabez* was a curiosity to me. How could so much be made of such a short passage of Scripture when so much of the Bible presents a contrasting view? Jabez asked God for several things, culminating in a request that he be spared from pain (1 Chronicles 4:10). The story has a seemingly happy ending, for the verse ends with these words: "And God granted his request." But what did Jabez do with his pain-free life? We don't know. All we know is that God didn't consider it worth

> I sometimes question my crusade to improve the image of pain. In a society that routinely portrays pain as the enemy, will anyone listen to a contrarian message extolling its virtues?
>
> —Philip Yancey

writing about. In the margin of my Bible I wrote: "And Jabez was never heard from again." Like Jabez, I want to be spared from pain. But in case after case throughout Scripture, God did His most remarkable work through people tested and tried and strengthened in the heat and pressure of pain and persecution. I am not suggesting that it is wrong to pray for relief from pain. Even Jesus prayed that God might have a Plan B in mind that would allow Him to avoid suffering. But in submitting to the will of His Father He made it possible for you and me to avoid eternal suffering.

Many people I know are suffering unimaginable losses. One lost the ability to perform routine tasks as the result of treatment for a brain tumor. One lost all mobility in an accident. Others have lost children. But their testimonies of praise prove that God's strength is being made perfect in their weakness. Even though they never would have chosen their circumstances, they know that God loves them and thus they are confident that He wants what ✳ is good *for* them and wants to accomplish good *through* them. They are experiencing what the apostle Paul wrote about: "I delight in weaknesses, in insults, in hardships, in persecutions, in difficulties. For when I am weak, then I am strong" (2 Corinthians 12:10). This is not easy to do. It requires unshakeable faith in the loving character of God.

Record For Brother Roger

When I was a child, I wondered why we thanked God for our food *before* eating it rather than after. In my immature mind, gratitude was simply a polite response after receiving something good, not the anticipation of receiving it. In the human realm, my thinking was logical. We risk embarrassment if we thank someone for a gift we have not yet received. But the situation with God is different. (We have His assurance that He desires to give us good gifts. So even when we receive something that doesn't seem good, we treat it like a package that is only partially open. We are grateful because we know there is more to it than we can see.

Praise is not a natural response in times of fear and uncertainty. It is supernatural. The world witnessed this when two Michigan families became the focus of media attention after an accident killed five people from Taylor University and seriously injured one other. The family of Whitney Cerak grieved the loss of their daughter, and the family of Laura VanRyn kept a bedside vigil praying for their daughter's full recovery and watching for any signs that she was emerging from unconsciousness. Five weeks after the accident, in a reversal that stunned not only those involved but the entire nation, Laura's family realized that the young woman they had been watching over was not their daughter but her classmate Whitney. Although neither family spoke publicly, they posted blogs that were like modern day psalms. When attacked by Satan's cruelest weapon, both families fought back with praise. Even their laments were punctuated with exclamations proclaiming their certainty of God's goodness. In their final blog, Laura's family quoted 1 Peter 1:3-7:

> Praise be to the God and Father of our Lord Jesus Christ! In his great mercy he has given us new birth into a living hope through the resurrection of Jesus Christ from the dead, and into an inheritance that can never perish, spoil or fade—kept in heaven for you, who through faith are shielded by God's power until the coming of the salvation that is ready to be

revealed in the last time. In this you greatly rejoice, though now for a little while you may have had to suffer grief in all kinds of trials. These have come so that your faith—of greater worth than gold, which perishes even though refined by fire—may be proved genuine and may result in praise, glory and honor when Jesus Christ is revealed.

Praise is exercise for the heart. We start when we are weak, and it makes us strong—strong in the Lord. The certainty that God's ways are better than ours is where strength of heart begins.

The LORD is my strength and my shield; my heart trusts in him, and I am helped. My heart leaps for joy and I will give thanks to him in song.
—Psalm 28:7

The Strength of My Soul | Humility

After attending a funeral at church, I headed across the street to the college where I was teaching a section of freshman English. I was early, so I planned to sit in the café and study until time for class. I ordered a caramel latté and settled down to review my notes. I made a point of sitting where I had a clear view of the clock.

While I was studying, a woman I had not seen for a long time came in. She too had been to the funeral so we talked about the service and our friend whose husband had died in a plane crash. Then I told her about my class and how much I enjoyed the students. I kept checking the clock so I wouldn't be late. My class started at two o'clock, so I kept waiting for the minute hand to say "ten 'til." When I looked, it said "fifteen after," so I figured I had at least another thirty minutes before heading to class.

As we were talking, one of my students walked up to our table. I smiled at him and introduced him to my friend. Then he handed me a stack of papers.

"What's this?" I asked.

"Our assignments that were due today," he said.

"Why are you giving them to me now?" I asked.

"Because you never came to class," he explained.

"What do you mean? I'm right here." I looked at the clock again. The minute hand said twenty after. To me that meant I had forty minutes before class started.

"Class starts at two," he said. "It's twenty after."

I realized then that I had been so focused on the minute hand that I was not seeing the hour hand.

"Why didn't someone come and get me?" I asked.

"We didn't know you were here until just about everyone had left," he said.

I wanted to believe him because I wanted to think the best about the young Christian students preparing to take my place in the ranks of Christendom when my time expires. But I remembered myself at their age, so I had some sizeable doubts. Besides, the café where I was sitting was located below a balcony just outside my classroom, and I suspected that my students had been watching from above and waiting for the college-mandated twenty minutes to pass so they could legitimately consider the class canceled without the risk of being marked absent.

At that moment, however, finding out the truth about my students was less important than <u>finding out the truth about myse</u>lf. I recalled some of the words we'd been discussing and writing about. One of the words was *anonymity*, which was appropriate because I definitely did not want my name attached to this incident. Even though

I couldn't keep the secret from my students, I immediately started plotting a way to keep it from my husband. Jay understands how things like clocks and numbers work and is somehow able to make them work *for* him. With me, they are more belligerent, and I always feel like a failure when I can't get them to cooperate.

Failure was another word we had discussed. Just a week earlier, I had handed back some papers with rather disappointing grades. After letting the shock set in, I gave my students a cheerful little speech about how we often learn more from our failure than from our success. My plan, however, was for them to learn from *their own* failure, not from mine. I prefer not to have God use me as a bad example.

Jesus Christ can afford to be misunderstood; we cannot. Our weakness lies in always wanting to vindicate ourselves.

—Oswald Chambers

To avoid telling Jay this new story about my inability to live in real time, I decided that I would adopt the "don't ask, don't tell" policy. That way I wouldn't have to lie, and he wouldn't have to know. It sounded like a win-win solution. But on Saturday while we were driving home from an all-day choir workshop, Jay suddenly asked, "How did your class go on Friday?" Without a moment's hesitation I said, "Fine."

I'm not sure which surprised me more: How quickly the lie came to my lips or how quickly the rationalization came to my mind. *It wasn't really a lie,* I told myself. *The class really did "go" well. The whole class "went" right out the door.*

As soon as the word escaped from my mouth it started ringing in my ears. Even though I had redefined the word *lie* to absolve myself of guilt, I knew I was still guilty of deceit.

I put off the confession as long as I could, but the next morning on our way to church, as we neared the place where I had told the lie, I finally spoke the truth.

Our marriage survived, but my ego spent quite some time in recovery.

My reason for telling this story is to illustrate how difficult confession is. If it's so hard to confess such a small thing because it's personally humiliating, the likelihood that I will have the courage to admit when I am wrong about something of more consequence is remote.

I prefer to have God use my strength rather than my weakness, but that's not His preference. He wants to show His strength, not mine, and His strength is impossible to see when I keep trying to impress others with mine.

Over the centuries, the entrance to Bethlehem's

Church of the Nativity has twice been made smaller. The purpose in the last case was to keep marauders from entering the basilica on horseback. The entrance now is referred to as the Door of Humility because visitors must bend down to enter.

As we age, bending our knees becomes increasingly difficult and painful—both physically and spiritually. In the physical realm, some people undergo knee replacement surgery. To avoid years of increasing pain and debilitating joint damage, they endure several weeks of agony.

Like physical knees, spiritual knees

We all have a lurking desire to be exhibitions for God, to be put, as it were, in His show room. Jesus does not want us to be specimens, He wants us to be so taken up with Him that we never think about ourselves, and the only impression left on others by our life is that Jesus Christ is having unhindered way.

—Oswald Chambers

become stiff over time. Years of stubborn pride and self-centeredness make us inflexible, and it becomes increasingly difficult and painful for us to humble ourselves. Seduced by false feelings of importance when others submit to us, we never learn that true importance comes from submitting ourselves to God and others (Ephesians 5:21; 1 Peter 5:5).

The Door of Humility at the Church of the Nativity reminds us that we all need new knees—knees that will bend. The replacement procedure is painful, but it's the only way anyone can enter the presence of God.

In church we sometimes sing "Holy Is the Lord" by Chris Tomlin. When we get to the words "We stand and lift up our hands for the joy of the Lord is our strength," several people stand up. By the time we get to the next phrase, the whole congregation is standing. But the next phrase is "We bow down and worship Him now." I have yet to see anyone bow down when we sing those words. But the truth is, none of us can stand without first bowing down.

Bowing is difficult because it's associated with humility and everyone has a hard time with that. But imagine how effective our churches would be if the strength to bow down was as common as the courage to stand up.

The only real strength any of us have is God's. And the only official act of strength God asks that we perform on our own is to humble ourselves. Doing so is the solution to the basic human condition inherited from Adam and Eve. The book of Genesis states that we have fallen

You give me your shield of victory, and your right hand sustains me; you stoop down to make me great.

—Psalm 18:35

The LORD upholds all
those who fall and lifts up
all who are bowed down.

—Psalm 145:14

and we can't get up. The rest of Scripture outlines the simple but difficult solution: The only way to get up is to bow down!

The Strength of My Mind | Unity

I once decorated a notebook with definitions of the words *idea, thought, opinion, preference, belief,* and *conviction* to remind myself that they are not synonyms. My certainty is misplaced when I am overconfident of my own opinions. I'd rather not admit this, but I seldom look for God's promised way of escape when I am tempted to elevate my preferences to the level of convictions.

Scripture says that we need to subjugate even our beliefs and convictions to the law of love (Romans 13:8, 10; Galatians 5:14; James 2:8), for love transcends all other laws and leads to

If you think you are standing firm, be careful that you don't fall! No temptation has seized you except what is common to man. And God . . . will not let you be tempted beyond what you can bear . . . so that you can stand up under it.

—1 Corinthians 10:11-13

27

peace and mutual edification. Whenever opinions and preferences become more important to us than what God says is true, important, and valuable to Him, we have made idols out of our own beliefs.

Idolatry is the most serious offense in the Bible because it violates the first and most important command: "You shall have no other gods before me" (Exodus 20:3). An idol is more than a carved or forged image. It's a symbol of everything that the god stands for (or in most cases "falls for").

The Bible is filled with stories of people who go to all kinds of trouble to create and care for gods that are worse than helpless—they're needy! False gods fall over and have to be set upright. They have to be carried from place to place (or washed or cleaned or put away; or, in the case of opinions and preferences, defended). They are a burden. But people would rather cater to the gods they create than bow down to the One who created them. People work tirelessly to appease false gods but refuse to do the one thing that will make them acceptable to the one true God: bow down.

Few people are willing to set aside personal preferences for the sake of peace and mutual edification, but that's what Paul encouraged believers in Corinth to do: "I appeal to you, brothers, in the name of our Lord Jesus Christ, that all of you agree with one another so that there may be no divisions among you and that you may be perfectly united in mind and thought" (1 Corinthians 1:10).

When our choir director raised his baton to begin the song, we lowered our heads to focus on our music. He established the tempo, keeping the rhythm with his arms. To please him, we tried hard to sing the song perfectly, paying close attention to each note as we moved through the score.

After several bars, the director's arms began moving more emphatically. We looked more closely at our music, trying even harder to get the words and notes right. But he seemed increasingly displeased.

What was evident to the choir director slowly became obvious to the rest of us. We were singing the right notes, but we weren't together. Each of us had our own tempo—each slightly different from his. Technically speaking the gap was small—a mere split second—but artistically it was a gaping hole.

If you have any encouragement from being united with Christ, if any comfort from his love, if any fellowship with the Spirit, if any tenderness and compassion, then make my joy complete by being like-minded, having the same love, being one in spirit and purpose.

—Philippians 2:1-2

30

Realizing that no amount of frantic waving was going to get us together, he dropped his arms to his sides and stood motionless. We continued to sing, however, our heads buried in our music, unaware that he had stopped. Our eyes kept moving methodically from one note to the next, but the more we struggled to get ourselves together, the more disconnected we became.

Then gradually, one by one, our voices went silent as we realized that we were singing without a conductor. When at last the rehearsal room was quiet, he spoke. "You've got to get your noses out of your books," he pleaded. "We've been rehearsing this music for weeks. You know it better than you think you do. You've got to watch me. I know which parts give you trouble. Trust me to give you the cues. When you keep your noses in the book, you sing like robots. You have no life, no enthusiasm, no passion. You can't get energy out of the book; you've got to get it from me."

He was right, of course. The music improved significantly when we all trusted him to lead us.

Since then I have wondered if something similar is going on in heaven. Could it be that Jesus is waiting for us to realize what a confused mess we're in so we will stop our futile striving long enough to hear Him say, "You've studied my Word for years. You know it better than you think you do. It's time to look at Me. I know there's security in having words in front of you, but you've got the Word inside you. Looking at words on a page may keep you from making a few mistakes, but it won't keep you together. Only I can do that—and only if you keep your eyes on Me. Keeping your nose in the book will help you get the words right, but there won't be any energy or power because we won't be together. Words convey truth, but only I can give life."

I'm not suggesting that we ought *not* bury our noses in the Book. Certainly there is a time for that. But there is also a time for looking unto Jesus, the author and perfecter of our faith (Hebrews 12:2). God said that He would put His laws in our hearts and minds (Jeremiah 31:33; Hebrews 10:16). When His Word is part of us, it becomes obvious to others in the way we live.

"A new command I give you: Love one another. As I have loved you, so you must love one another. By this all men will know that you are my disciples, if you love one another."

—John 13:34-35

Good musicians don't need to hold up their music to prove they're singing correctly; their performance is proof enough. And Christians don't need an assortment of all-occasion Bible verses to prove we are right; our lives should be proof enough. The proof that we are "right," Jesus said, is our unity.

On the night He was betrayed, Jesus prayed for Himself, for His disciples, and for us. His prayer for those who would believe in Him through the message of the disciples included this request: "I pray . . . that all of them may be one, Father, just as you are in me and I am in you.

And over all these virtues put on love, which binds them all together in perfect unity.

—Colossians 3:14

May they also be in us so that the world may believe that you have sent me. I have given them the glory that you gave me, that they may be one as we are one: I in them and you in me. May they be brought to complete unity to let the world know that you sent me and have loved them even as you have loved me" (John 17:21-23).

The Strength of My Life | Integrity

One day in college our professor opened class with an unusual prayer:

> Humpty Dumpty sat on a wall
>
> Humpty Dumpty had a great fall
>
> All the king's horses and all the king's men
>
> Couldn't put Humpty together again.

We were surprised to hear our Shakespeare professor praying a nursery rhyme, but he ended with these words: "Thank you, Lord, that you can do what kings cannot— you *can* put Humpty Dumpty together again."

Thankfully, he was right, for we are all Humpty Dumptys. None of the bonding agents the world has produced can mend our brokenness. No matter how much self-repair we do, we remain broken and unable to pull ourselves together.

We sometimes use the word "together" to refer to someone who appears perfect. When we say, "She's so 'together,'" we mean that her nail polish and lipstick and purse and shoes and jewelry and clothes are perfectly coordinated. God's idea of having it "together" is different. He intends that our hearts, souls, minds, and bodies all be fitted together in Him. In other words, He wants us to have integrity. The word *integrity* comes from the word *integer*, which means "whole" or "complete." A synonym in Scripture is "perfect." When Jesus said "you are to be perfect as your heavenly Father is perfect," He used the Greek word *teleios*, which also means complete. Jesus wants to make us whole by making us one with Him, one with ourselves, and one with others.

In *Walking Away from Faith*, author Ruth Tucker tells the stories of those who once claimed to be Christians but later abandoned the faith. In many cases the "god" these people walked away from was an incomplete god. Those raised in austere, legalistic environments easily walk away from a god who is always angry and demanding. Those raised in homes where god is more of an intellectual idea than a living, loving being find other "ideas" more intriguing and satisfying. Those who know God as their best "buddy," leave Him when human buddies provide companionship more to their liking, perhaps by endorsing their sin or weaknesses. Those whose god is only a reflection of their own image are fascinated for a time, but only a narcissist can have a long-lasting relationship with his or her own image.

And let endurance have its perfect result, so that you may be perfect and complete, lacking in nothing.

—James 1:4 NASB

In other words, a god who is not whole is easy to leave behind. Whenever certain aspects of God are emphasized and others excluded, we end up with an incomplete god who is not worthy of worship. As beings who are created in His image, we need to beware of the temptation to worship an image of God that most closely resembles ourselves. Emotional people can be tempted to worship an emotional god. Intellectual people can be tempted to worship an intellectual god. Socially minded people can be tempted to worship a "do-good" god. God is all of those things and more, but He is not any one of them alone.

The Greatest Commandment begins with the phrase: "Hear, O Israel: the LORD our God, the LORD is one" (Deuteronomy 6:4). It is followed by the command to love God with all our heart, soul, and strength, which indicates that we are *not* one (6:5). We are in parts. The aspects of our being—heart, soul, mind, and flesh—were broken apart when Adam and Eve plunged headlong into sin. Since that moment, ominously referred to as "The Fall," humanity has been in pieces, and all of us have been making vain attempts to repair ourselves. God's plan of redemption is to put us back together again. Apart from Him, it cannot be done.

> Finally, be strong in the Lord and in his mighty power.
>
> —Ephesians 6:10

At my annual physical exam, my doctor asked his usual probing question. "Any problems with your health this year?"

For years I had given the same answer. "No, just colds and stuff." But that year I had my list ready.

"Well, I've been slowing down a lot this year," I said.

"And when I sit on the floor, I have a hard time getting up again."

"That's pretty normal for your age," he said. "It's just going to get worse. If there's anything you want to do, do it now."

"Thanks," I said. "I'll call you the next time I need encouragement."

He smiled and then continued his speech. "Exercise would help. At your age it's more important than ever to maintain motion. If you don't exercise your muscles, your joints have to do all the heavy work, and that causes a lot of stress. Anything else bothering you?"

"Yes. I'm always cold and tired and I've been gaining weight. Are there some vitamins or something I could take to speed up my metabolism?"

"No. You just need more exercise. Exercise develops

muscle, and muscle burns more calories than fat. Anything else?"

"Yes. Do you know anything about shoulders?" I wasn't trying to insult him, but he's a gynecologist, and I didn't know how much time he'd spent studying the skeletal system.

"I broke mine a couple years ago," he said. "I learned something then. What's your problem?"

"I think it's out of joint or something. I'm wondering if I should go to a chiropractor."

I demonstrated my limited range of motion, and then he tugged and pulled my arm into positions that caused my eyes to squeeze shut in pain.

Finally he announced his diagnosis. "Tendonitis," he said. "You're going to have to work it out. It'll be very painful, but if you don't do it your shoulder will freeze up.

Then you'll have to go to physical therapy, which will be even more painful—and costly."

While demonstrating what I needed to do, he explained, "Poke around until you find the place that hurts the most. That's the injured tendon. Massage it as hard as you can as you move your arm. It will feel like a knife going through your shoulder, but that's what it will take to loosen it up."

As I did the recommended shoulder exercises, I recalled these words: "Exercise yourself toward godliness, for bodily discipline is only of little profit, but godliness is profitable for all things, since it holds promise for the present life and also for the life to come" (1 Timothy 4:7 NKJV; 4:8 NASB). While paying the price for neglecting physical exercise, I was reminded that it's even worse to neglect spiritual exercise.

When it comes to physical health, we believe experts who tell us that exercise is important. Yet we are slow to believe that spiritual exercise is essential for spiritual health. Those who join a sports team expect to put in long hours of practice, and no right-minded coach would put a player into a game who doesn't know the rules. Why, then, do we expect God to use us for something great even though we live on the spiritual equivalent of junk food, read the Bible as if it were a good luck charm, and seldom attempt to practice what it says we're to do? We know that being a spectator will not get us into any sports hall of fame. Yet we sit on the spiritual sidelines and expect to become strong in the Lord. To accomplish the mighty things God wants to do in and through us, we have to do difficult things through Him.

Physical and spiritual exercise have this in common:

If one part suffers, every part suffers with it; if one part is honored, every part rejoices with it.

—1 Corinthians 12:26

both are painful. Both require us to do something that at least one part of our body does not want to do. In the case of physical exercise, our flesh says to our mind: "This hurts. If you really loved me, you wouldn't make me do it." The mind of course knows that the opposite is true. Demanding that the flesh do something painful is actually proof of love. In order for our bodies to work properly, our minds and hearts must be in agreement as to what is good, and our bodies must submit.

In the spiritual realm, because of our broken condition, every part looks out for its own self-interest and has the ability to give the other parts bad advice. For example, faulty thinking about our self-image might cause our mind to assert undue control and refuse our body the food it needs to maintain health. Or faulty desires may take control and refuse to give up a relationship that our mind knows is bad for us. Or physical cravings may take control and refuse to give up a substance or behavior that is destructive.

Satan has an alarming ability to exploit our weaknesses by exaggerating our strengths. He convinces us that we are good, not God; that our way is right, not God's; that our thoughts are reasonable, not God's; that our feelings are valid, not God's. Exercise in godliness is required to combat these deadly deceptions.

In the realm of physical fitness, expert Greg Landry gives this advice: "Look for the 'hard' way to do things." This is like the spiritual advice Jesus gave when He said we are to love our enemies and do good to those who hate us (Luke 6:27). Being kind to those who are nice requires little spiritual strength—even pagans can do it, Jesus said. But being kind to our enemies requires spiritual training equivalent to that of an Olympic athlete. We can't do it without spiritual coaching, lots of practice, and even lots of bumps and bruises.

Spiritual exercise, like its physical counterpart, requires that we do what feels bad to maintain good health. Like learning to hide the good that I do (Matthew 6:3-4) and reveal the bad (James 5:16). Like praising God when it seems as if I'm losing. Like humbling myself when I'm certain I should be exalted. Like giving up my pet preference for the sake of unity in my community of believers. Like putting others ahead of myself, forgiving those who hurt me, being kind to those who hate me, and not returning evil for evil.

One of the most difficult situations in which to exercise these virtues is when a once-loving relationship becomes spite-filled and vindictive. A spouse leaves us with a mound of debt and diminishing self-esteem. An adult child mocks our faith and belittles our values. An angry family member turns others in the family against us.

Those who say "sticks and stones may break my bones but names will never hurt me" must never have experienced the intense emotional pain of a failed dream, a broken relationship, or a personal attack. Snubs, slurs, slights, and insults make us feel as if we've been kicked in the stomach. They are as cruel as any physical blow, and they leave us feeling weak and helpless. The pain is even worse when inflicted by someone we love, or someone we thought loved us, or someone we trusted with our kindness or generosity.

King David experienced this kind of pain when his son Absalom led a rebellion to claim the throne. With his family divided and his army in disarray, David fled Jerusalem, weeping as he went. Along the way he encountered Shimei, a member of Saul's family, who shouted curses at him. David's men wanted to kill Shimei, but David stopped them. "Leave him alone," David said, "It may be that the LORD will see my distress and repay me with good for the cursing I am receiving today" (2 Samuel 16:11-12).

Most people are happy when someone offers to get vengeance on their behalf. But David realized that something bigger was going on. Although he did not stick around to suffer more abuse, he was aware that God might have a purpose for it and that good could come out of it if he refused to return evil for evil.

Whenever we are being treated unjustly, it's good to remember that God may intend to repay us with good. In his letter to Christians living in Rome, the apostle Paul wrote, "Do not be overcome by evil, but overcome evil with good" (Romans 12:21). Goodness often seems like a wimpy weapon against the forces of evil, but many have used it with great effectiveness.

Goodness is the only investment which never fails.

—Henry David Thoreau

Ken Sande, the founder of Peacemaker Ministries and author of *The Peacemaker*, gives this advice:

> When someone has wronged you, it is also helpful to remember that God is sovereign and loving. Therefore, when you are having a hard time forgiving that person, take time to note how God may be using the offense for good. Is this

When wronged remember

an unusual opportunity to glorify God? How can you serve others and help them grow in their faith? What sins and weaknesses of yours are being exposed for the sake of your growth? What character qualities are you being challenged to exercise? When you perceive that the person who has wronged you is being used as an instrument in God's hand to help you mature, serve others, and glorify him, it may be easier for you to move ahead with forgiveness. —Ken Sande, *The Peacemaker*

I have a friend whose husband stole money from his employer. To avoid criminal prosecution, he agreed to pay it back. For several years, most of my friend's paycheck went to pay off the debt. Sadly, her husband continued his deceptive behavior and they eventually divorced. Due to state divorce laws, my friend was ordered to pay half the remaining debt. She couldn't afford to keep the family home, so she moved into an apartment. After several difficult job situations, she found a position that fits her interests and abilities, and God is moving her toward wholeness. Through it all, she never spoke badly to her children about their father. Even when they blamed her for the breakup of their family, she refused to say or do anything to damage their relationship with their dad. Her ex-husband filed for bankruptcy to avoid paying his half of the debt. She is still paying her half. Her children now admire her for letting the truth reveal itself rather than revealing it to them in an attempt to vindicate herself.

I look at my friend with great admiration. She refused to return evil for evil, and God is now rewarding her with good. In one of his songs, David wrote, "Be still and know that I am God" (Psalm 46:10). My friend did the hard work of being still, and she has come to know God in an amazing new way through the work He has done on her behalf.

Choosing to follow God will take us through some tight and uncomfortable places. The Bible is full of examples of people whom God purified and strengthened by pressing them through the narrow way of affliction.

Being hurt by a friend or loved one is bad enough, but what if God Himself takes away His hand of protection? That's what happened to Job. And not because he did something bad, but because he was good—so good in fact that God said of him: "There is no one on earth like him; he is blameless and upright, a man who fears God and shuns evil" (Job 1:8).

Job is the only person mentioned in the Bible whom God identified as having integrity. The Lord said to Satan,

Job "still maintains his integrity, though you incited me against him to ruin him without any reason" (2:3). In a short space of time, Job lost everything dear to him: his children were killed, his wealth disintegrated, his good name was tarnished, his closest friends suspected him of wrongdoing, and his wife considered him foolish for not turning against God. Eventually even Job's health was taken from him. Job's distress was so great that he pleaded, "May the day of my birth perish" (3:3). Job wanted God to erase all memory of his existence! He had enjoyed years of success and respect. Without those, he questioned the purpose of living (3:20). "The thing I greatly feared has come upon me," he said (3:25). We could say that Job had *all* of our worst fears come upon him.

Job wanted to die and be forgotten, but instead God made sure his name and story would be remembered forever. Rather than give Job what he asked for, God gave future generations what they would need—an inside look at the spiritual battle between God and Satan. The result is a document of God's thoughts about suffering that has comforted countless people.

When Satan attacks us with his most powerful weapons and the thing we greatly fear comes upon us, we know, thanks to Job, that God can use our suffering for good. Through it, He can strengthen us and perhaps future generations as well.

Suffering is the narrow way that leads to spiritual life and strength, for it is through suffering that we are prepared for eternal glory: "And the God of all grace, who called you to his eternal glory in Christ, after you have suffered a little while, will himself restore you and make you strong, firm and steadfast" (1 Peter 5:10). script

Everyday life in a broken world provides plenty of opportunities for exercise in godliness. But what is a good exercise routine? In his second letter, the apostle Peter gives an answer. He says, in fact, that if we do these things we will never fall (2 Peter 1:10):

> Make every effort to add to your faith goodness;
> and to goodness, knowledge; and to knowledge,
> self-control; and to self-control, perseverance;
> and to perseverance, godliness; and to godliness,
> brotherly kindness; and to brotherly kindness, love.
> —2 Peter 1:5-7

The order in which these attributes are listed is not coincidental. When we consider their meanings and implications, we see a progression.

Goodness is the desire to do the right thing. It is first because it marks the starting place of faith. Everything we do, good and bad, begins with desire. The desire to do what is right, therefore, is the first step in our relationship with God.

Knowledge, the ability to discern what is right, comes second because doing the right thing requires that we first figure out what right is.

Self-control, the resolve to do the right thing, comes next. Without steadfast determination, we will be tempted to change our minds when we find out that doing right is often very difficult.

Perseverance, the endurance to keep doing the right thing, is self-control running the Boston Marathon. To persevere means that we continually control our passions and repeatedly act in accord with our knowledge of what ought to be done rather than give in to what we feel like doing.

Godliness, the goal of doing the right thing, is an attitude we're to develop as our behavior improves. The danger that lurks in doing right is pride. When we begin moving toward spiritual maturity, the Enemy will try to make us believe that our improvement is due to our own efforts and for our own personal benefit. Godliness, however, is unselfishness. A godly person does the right thing not for selfish gain but so that the plan of God will be revealed and others might see a living example of how much better it is to follow God's way.

Brotherly kindness, the means of doing the right thing, is the tangible expression of godliness revealed through acts of thoughtfulness, generosity, honesty, and concern.

Love, the highest motive for doing the right thing, extends God's goodness to everyone, including the undeserving and even our enemies. We talk flippantly about loving God and loving one another, the commandment that Jesus says is the most important of all because it summarizes and incorporates all the others. But seen from this perspective, with a view of all the work that must precede genuine love, it becomes apparent that what we call love is often a pathetic substitute.

Although these attributes build on one another, we don't have to become perfect in one before working on the next. In *How Do You Live the Christian Life*, Mart De Haan wrote, "The seven steps . . . show us the logic and progression of real faith. They show us that God is not just looking for love or faith or knowledge. He's looking for all these characteristics as they combine to provide a complete, balanced, progressive Christian experience."

As we add these exercises to our routine, we "participate in the divine nature and escape the corruption in the world caused by evil desires" (2 Peter 1:4). Script

The difference between physical and spiritual exercise is that physical exercise stalls the inevitable—death by corruption—whereas through spiritual exercise we participate in the divine (incorruptible) nature and thus prepare for eternity.

None of us can avoid the evidence of social corruption and moral decay. Nor can we ignore the people desperate for an escape. God has provided the way out, and Peter has mapped the journey like a spiritual Mapquest. The way is narrow. At times, we may feel claustrophobic and be tempted to turn back. But following it is

> The love of God in Christ Jesus is such that He can take the most unfit man—unfit to survive, unfit to fight, unfit to face moral issues— and make him not only fit to survive and to fight, but fit to face the biggest moral issues and the strongest power of Satan, and come off more than a conqueror.
> —Oswald Chambers

the only way to escape the corruption ourselves and to lead others out of it.

To some, faith is no more than an intense form of wishing. But real faith is work. It's our work. And our faith is God's work. He is making our lives a work of art that will attract worshipers into His kingdom.

When we start with the mistaken belief that faith makes life easy, we waste energy and suffer frustration trying to make our faulty belief true. But once we concede that faith is hard work, we are free to use our energy in productive ways. Instead of wasting it on futile attempts to achieve an easy life, we can invest it in the productive pursuit of a good life. The strength gained from living a good life eventually makes life easier as well because God's strength is perfected in us.

I am not the Martha type. God must have been

thinking about something other than domestic skills when I was formed in His mind. But I know a few basics. I know that getting rid of stains and wrinkles requires heat and pressure. The Bible uses this domestic metaphor when describing Christ's relationship to His bride, the church.

> Christ loved the church and gave himself up for her to make her holy, cleansing her by the washing with water through the word, and to present her to himself as a radiant church, without stain or wrinkle or any other blemish, but holy and blameless.
>
> —Ephesians 5:25-27

Having started with the engagement metaphor, it is fitting to end with a wedding metaphor. The same things that produce the symbol of love, a diamond, also produce the object of love, the bride herself. Heat and pressure are required to make us holy and radiant. The purity formed in us through adversity is the strength of Christ made perfect in us. To love God with all our strength is to find all our strength in Him.

Even the most perfectly cut and polished diamond has no beauty on its own. Without one essential component, a diamond looks much like other rocks. A diamond's beauty depends on light. A diamond in the dark is ordinary. Light makes all the difference.

The LORD is my light and my salvation—whom shall I fear? The LORD is the stronghold of my life—of whom shall I be afraid?

—Psalm 27:1

Glorious God and loving Father, may every desire, every breath, every thought, and every deed be for Your glory. Fit us for heaven through our afflictions on earth. May Your strength be formed in us through the purifying forces You use in our lives. May our purity enable the light of Your love to radiate through us with such amazing

beauty that all the world is attracted to the splendor of
Your holiness. We are indebted to You for all things
and to You all honor and glory and power belong.
Amen.

This is what the Sovereign LORD,
the Holy One of Israel, says:
"In repentance and rest is your
salvation, in quietness and trust is
your strength." —Isaiah 30:15

To him who is able

to keep you from falling

and to present you before

his glorious presence without

fault and with great joy—to

the only God our Savior be

glory, majesty, power and

authority, through Jesus Christ

our Lord, before all ages,

now and forevermore! Amen.

—Jude 1:24-25